What on Earth? Tornadoes

What on Earth?

What's this?

Turn this page to find out!

First published in 2005 by
Book House an imprint of
The Salariya Book Company
25 Marlborough Place
Brighton
BN1 1UB

Please visit The Salariya Book Company at: **www.salariya.com**

HB ISBN 1-905087-35-7
PB ISBN 1-905087-36-5

Visit our website at **www.book-house.co.uk**
for free electronic versions of:
You Wouldn't Want To Be An Egyptian Mummy!
You Wouldn't Want To Be A Roman Gladiator!
You Wouldn't Want to Sail on a 19th-Century Whaling Ship!
Avoid joining Shackleton's Polar Expedition!

Due to the changing nature of internet links, The Salariya Book Company has
developed an online list of websites related to the subject of this book.
This site is updated regularly. Please use this link to access the list:
http://www.book-house.co.uk/WOE/tornadoes

A catalogue record for this book is available from the British Library.

Printed and bound in China.

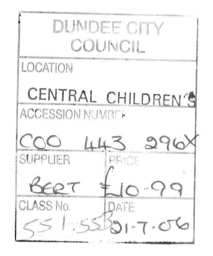

Editors: Ronald Coleman
                             Sophie Izod
Senior Art Editor: Carolyn Franklin
DTP Designer: Mark Williams

Picture Credits Julian Baker & Janet Baker
(J B Illustrations): 6-7, 8(t), 9(t) 10-11, Nick Hewetson: 9(b),
15(t), Corbis: 8, 13, 25, 28, 29, 31, Digital Vision: 16, 26,
TOPEX/Poseidon Team/CNES/NASA: 18, John Shaw/NHPA: 18
Dr. Joseph Golden/NOAA: 3, 23, National Weather Service
Forecast Office Albany NY: 12, NOAA Photo Library/NOAA
Central Library/OAR/ERL/NSSL: 1, 14, 17, National Weather
Service Forecast Office Knoxville TN: 15, NOAA/ Historic
NWS Collection: 22, Topfoto.co.uk: 21

Cover credit: Corbis

What on Earth?

Bang!
It's a giant hailstone.
Tornadoes often happen at
the same time as
thunderstorms, heavy rain
and huge hailstones.

Crack! Bang! Flash!

What on Earth? Tornadoes

DAVID AND HELEN ORME

What do we call a tornado over the sea?

Turn to page 22 to find out!

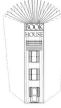

BOOK HOUSE

Contents

What on Earth?

Raining frogs?

Sometimes, a tornado scoops up frogs or fish and carries them into the sky. They may surprise people by coming down in the rain far away.

Introduction

A tornado is a wind that spins around very fast, forming a shape like a funnel. Tornadoes are very dangerous, but mainly because they pick up huge amounts of debris – pieces of buildings, trees, bits of metal and even whole cars. The biggest danger from a tornado is getting hit by some of this.

Where are the most tornadoes?

Three out of four of all the world's tornadoes happen in the United States. There is a part of the United States where tornadoes are so common that people call it 'Tornado Alley'.

How fast can a tornado go?

Tornadoes are the fastest winds on the planet. The very fastest ones can spin at over 402 kilometres (250 miles) per hour.

What happens in a tornado?

As the tornado spins, it moves along the ground, sucking air into the bottom and forcing it upwards. Powerful tornadoes are like giant vacuum cleaners, sucking up objects such as cars or even buildings, causing great destruction. It is not the same thing as a hurricane. Tornado winds are much faster but they don't usually travel as far or cause as much damage as a hurricane.

How big are they?

Most tornadoes are small. A typical tornado makes a damage path 46 metres (50 yards) wide and 1.6 to 3.2 kilometres (1 to 2 miles) long. The largest tornado path can be 1.6 kilometres (1 mile) wide. The damage path can be as long as 161 kilometres (100 miles)!

Anvil-shaped thundercloud

Hailstones

Rain

Funnel (vortex)

What on Earth?

Flat-top?

Thunderclouds have a flat top. Some people say that a thundercloud looks like a blacksmith's anvil.

7

Where do tornadoes happen?

Tornadoes can happen anywhere, but they are most common in the United States, and also in India and Bangladesh. These are also the places where the most **severe** tornadoes occur.

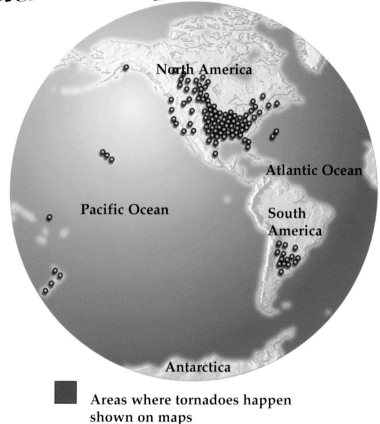

North America

Atlantic Ocean

Pacific Ocean

South America

Antarctica

Areas where tornadoes happen shown on maps

What time of day?

Tornadoes are most common in the late afternoon. All day, the sun has warmed the ground. As the air above begins to cool, hot air rises from the ground to meet it. When the warm air meets the cold air, a tornado may form.

Africa

Europe

Asia

India

Pacific Ocean

Indian Ocean

Australia

Antarctica

Although they happen throughout the year, in some places there are 'seasons' for tornadoes, especially in spring and early summer. These happen because of changing wind patterns at that time of year.

What is a twister?

Tornadoes (right) are also known as twisters or whirlwinds. The dark funnel-shaped column of a tornado moves along the ground at 32 to 113 kilometres (20 to 70 miles) per hour.

What happens next?

More and more warm air is sucked up into the clouds. A storm cell of slowly spinning cumulonimbus clouds can form. Sometimes, a fast spinning column of air forms inside this storm cell. This is called a **vortex**. If it reaches the ground, it is a tornado.

Winds at the upper level push the tornado along

Where do tornadoes get their energy from?

Thunderclouds are full of energy. The energy begins as something called latent heat which comes from the sun. This causes water from the sea to evaporate. When the water vapour cools and turns to water droplets, this energy is released and can cause high winds, thunderstorms, and tornadoes.

What on Earth?

Why do tornadoes spin?

When two winds move in different directions and at different speeds, the air between them spins. To see how, put a pencil between your hands. Move one hand towards you and one away from you. The pencil will spin!

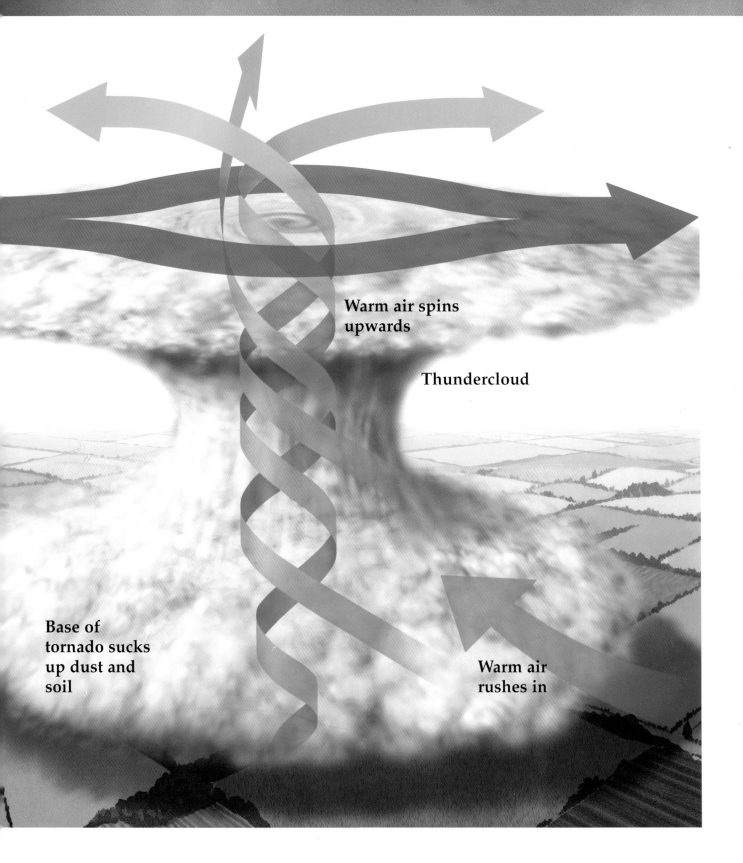

Warm air spins upwards

Thundercloud

Base of tornado sucks up dust and soil

Warm air rushes in

How do we measure a tornado?

Scientists use special equipment to measure the diameter of a tornado's funnel, how fast it travels, and how fast it spins. The most important measurement is how **fast** it is spinning, because the faster it spins, the more dangerous it is. Scientists estimate a tornado's speed from the damage it does.

Who was Professor Fujita?

Professor Theodore Fujita (1920-1998) invented the 'Fujita Scale' to estimate the speed a tornado spins. Category F0 with winds less than 117 kilometres (73 miles) per hour cause light damage.

F1, at 117-180 kilometres (73-112 miles) per hour, can push a car off the road. F5, at over 420 kilometres (260 miles) per hour can lift a house from its foundations.

Can tornadoes skip?

No they can't! Many people think that when a tornado doesn't touch the ground for a while it is 'skipping'. But a tornado that is not touching the ground is just a storm cell!

How are people warned?

It is impossible to forecast where a tornado might strike until it's very close. When forecasters think there is a risk, they give warnings on radio and television. In some areas, there are tornado sirens. When people hear these they should take shelter. However, because there are many false alarms, people may ignore these important warnings.

How does radar help predict tornadoes?

Radar uses radio signals which bounce off objects such as raindrops, and create a picture of the clouds. This helps forecasters work out what is happening inside a thundercloud and if a tornado is likely to form.

How do forecasters get information?

Weather forecasters analyse information from weather stations and then tell us what sort of weather we can expect.

Weather stations get information from satellites, weather balloons, aircraft and radar. But even with all the modern technology available, it is hard to tell exactly when and where a tornado will happen.

What on Earth? Who gets warnings?

The U.S. weather service is very experienced in predicting tornadoes, but in countries where tornadoes are rare, or where there isn't a good weather service, little or no warning is possible.

Who are Storm chasers?

Storm chasers are people who like to get as close as they can to storms and tornadoes. They may be scientists who study weather, or just people who enjoy the **excitement** of being close to one of nature's most amazing events. Some storm chasers earn a living by selling close-up photographs and videos of tornadoes.

What are they waiting for?

These chasers are waiting to photograph a tornado. They may have travelled hundreds of kilometres to see it.

What sort of equipment is used?

Many storm chasers use fast, safe vehicles, equipped with scientific instruments to measure wind speed, air pressure and humidity. They may even have portable radar.

How dangerous is it?

Very! The wind is dangerous, and so are heavy rain, hailstones and objects that tornadoes fling into the air.

What on Earth?

How big can a hailstone be?

The storms that create tornadoes can produce huge hailstones that weigh almost one kilogram (two pounds), which is the size of a grapefruit!

Where is Tornado Alley?

Tornado Alley is a large area of the United States where a great many tornadoes happen. It stretches from Texas in the south to North Dakota in the north, and east of the Rocky Mountains. There have been tornadoes in most American states.

Where are the Rocky Mountains?

The Rocky Mountains stretch from the south-west of the United States to north-west Canada in the far north.

Map showing Tornado Alley, North America

Labels on map: Montana, North Dakota, Minnesota, Wyoming, South Dakota, Iowa, Rocky Mountains, Nebraska, Colorado, Kansas, Missouri, New Mexico, Oklahoma, Arkansas, Texas

Why do tornadoes happen in Tornado Alley?

Weather systems over the Rocky Mountains pull in cold winds from Canada in the north. Warm winds from the south-east are full of water vapour from the ocean. These winds are pushed upwards when they reach the mountains, where they meet the cold air. These are perfect conditions for tornadoes to form.

What on Earth? Why are American tornadoes so violent?

Big land areas like North America have great extremes of temperature. This means that thunderstorms containing large amounts of energy and tornadoes are likely to form.

Where was the world's worst tornado?

Bangladesh is a poor country where most of the population are farmers. People must live where their crops grow, even if the area is in danger from floods and storms. They cannot escape easily as roads are rough making travel difficult. Their homes are quickly damaged and if crops are spoiled, there may be nothing else to eat. The world's **deadliest** tornado struck Bangladesh, a country to the east of India, in April, 1989. Over 1,300 people died and 50,000 lost their homes.

What on Earth? How long does a tornado last?

A tornado can last from several seconds to over an hour!

The photograph (right) shows the effect of a tornado on Bangladesh in 1991. A lot of people were able to use special storm shelters that had been built since the last major disaster. However, more than one and a half million homes were destroyed, and many people lost their lives.

Sandwip Island off the coast of Bangladesh, four days after the tornado hit

Can tornadoes happen at sea?

Tornadoes at sea are called 'waterspouts'. In fact, they are columns of water **vapour**, not water. Like tornadoes, they are usually formed by thunderstorms, when warm and cold air meet. They can happen anywhere, but are especially common in the seas around Florida in the United States.

How dangerous are waterspouts?

Waterspouts have less energy than land tornadoes. They do not pick up and throw objects but they can be powerful enough to damage or sink quite large boats. They aren't reported in tornado records unless they hit land.

What's the Bermuda Triangle?

It is an area of the Atlantic Ocean. Stories tell us that many ships have mysteriously disappeared there. Perhaps waterspouts are to blame.

Are tornadoes getting worse?

Many scientists believe that the world's weather is getting warmer. If the sea is warmer, the winds coming from it will have more energy. When this **energy** is released in thunderstorms, tornadoes will become stronger.

What's the evidence?

In the 1950s, around 500 were recorded each year in the USA. By the 1990s, the average was over 1,000 a year.

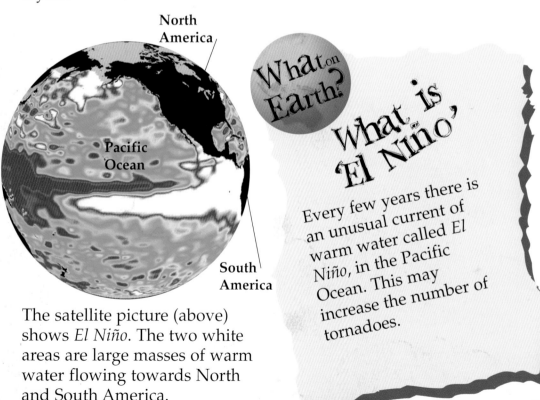

North America

Pacific Ocean

South America

The satellite picture (above) shows *El Niño*. The two white areas are large masses of warm water flowing towards North and South America.

What on Earth?

What is 'El Niño'

Every few years there is an unusual current of warm water called El Niño, in the Pacific Ocean. This may increase the number of tornadoes.

How strong is the evidence?

In the 1950s, scientists may not have known about tornadoes in remote areas. There may just seem to be more now because more are being detected. Tornadoes do more damage than in the past, but this may be because more land is covered by houses and factories.

What's the best kind of house to live in?

The best kind of house to live in is one specially built to survive tornadoes. Builders and architects are trying to create tornado-proof buildings. People in older homes can build 'safe rooms' inside their houses, make their basements safe, or build underground shelters. The worst kind of house to live in is a mobile home.

This house (below), was struck by a tornado. Its roof was blown away and its walls were blown down.

What on Earth? Good advice?

People used to open windows in case air pressure differences in a tornado made their house explode. This is not true, tornadoes can't make houses explode.

How would you survive a tornado?

If you go to a place where tornadoes are common, it is important to learn about how to stay safe. Everyone should know in advance what to do when a tornado hits. Don't wait until one is about to happen! Pay attention to weather forecasts, so you can be warned, and can head for safety.

Tornado Dangers

Outside The worst place to be when a tornado hits. Find shelter as quickly as possible.

Flying debris Kills the most amount of people during a tornado. Stay away from windows, doors and anything which is not pinned down.

Vehicles People often think they are safe in their cars or trucks, but tornadoes can pick them up killing the people inside. If you can, leave your vehicle and find a sturdy building.

Things to do Check-list

Learn to watch the weather in the sky. Look out for very dark storm clouds. Hail may be a sign a tornado is on its way, and so is rubbish falling from the sky. Learn to listen for tornadoes. You may hear a rushing sound, which gets louder. Look out for leaves being pulled upwards by the wind. Most of all, watch out for funnel-shaped clouds!

Keep a supply of candles and batteries for a torch in case the power goes out. Listen for warning sirens and move to a shelter immediately. If you can, wear a helmet, this may save your life if the roof caves in. If you can't move to a shelter, sit under a table and cover yourself with cushions and pillows to protect against flying debris.

27

Tornado facts

No one is quite sure where the word 'tornado' comes from. Some people say it is from two Spanish words, 'tronada' an old word for thunderstorm, and 'tornar', meaning to turn.

A tornado that hit Oklahoma city in May 1999 may have been an 'F6' with winds around 510 kilometres (320 miles) per hour. We can't be sure though, since there is no way to measure tornadoes more destructive than an F5.

You can go on a storm-chasing holiday. There are companies that promise to get visitors as close as possible to a tornado, then get them safely away again. It's more exciting than lying on a beach!

The sky sometimes turns a greenish colour before a tornado happens.

In 1915, in Kansas, USA, five horses and the rail they were tied to were carried 0.4 kilometres (0.25 miles) by a tornado and were found unhurt, still tied to the rail.

The longest recorded distance travelled by a tornado was an incredible 477 kilometres (293 miles), and happened in 1917.

Glossary

Bermuda Triangle An area in the Atlantic Ocean where ships and aircraft have disappeared.

Condense To turn from a gas to a liquid when cooled.

Cumulonimbus clouds Towering clouds with a flat base, seen in thunderstorms.

Current Water or air moving in a particular direction.

Diameter The distance across something circular, like the funnel of a tornado.

Estimate Use facts to make a guess.

Fujita Scale A scale invented by Professor Theodore Fujita to estimate the spin speed of a tornado by seeing how much damage it has caused.

Humidity The amount of water vapour in the air.

Hurricane A powerful tropical storm.

Latent heat The energy contained in water vapour which is released when it is cools.

Radar A way of detecting objects at a distance by making radio waves bounce off them.

Storm cell The rotating clouds in a thunderstorm.

Vortex A spinning column of air.

Water vapour Water in the form of a gas.

Weather balloon A balloon with equipment to measure weather conditions high in the atmosphere.

What do you know about tornadoes?

1   What is the difference between a tornado and a hurricane?

2   How fast does an F5 tornado spin?

3   Which country gets the most tornadoes?

4   Where is Tornado Alley?

5   How are people warned about possible tornadoes?

6   How do people protect themselves from tornadoes?

7   What should someone do if they are in a car when a tornado is coming?

8   What are tornadoes over the sea called?

9   Are there more tornadoes now than in the past?

10 What is the most dangerous thing about tornadoes?

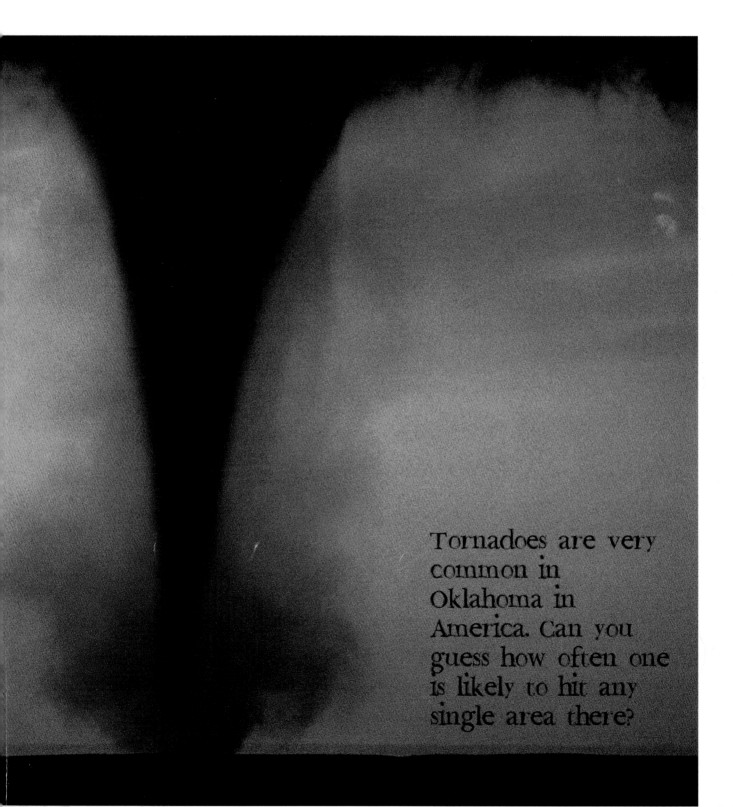

Tornadoes are very common in Oklahoma in America. Can you guess how often one is likely to hit any single area there?

Index

Pictures are shown in **bold.**

Answers

1   A hurricane is a violent tropical storm affecting a wide area. A tornado is faster, but affects a much smaller area. (See page 6)
2   At over 420 kilometres (260 miles) an hour. (See page 12)
3   The United States. (See page 5)
4   In the United States, stretching from Texas in the south to North Dakota in the north. (See page 18)
5   By radio and television, and in some places, warning sirens. (See page 14)
6   By building storm shelters, safe rooms or basements in their houses. (See page 26)
7   Leave the car and find shelter in a sturdy building. (See page 27)
8   Waterspouts. (See page 22)
9   We don't know. More are being recorded, but there may not actually be any more. (See page 25)
10 Objects being blown around. (See page 5)

Even in Oklahoma, a single area is only likely to be hit in exactly the same place once every 700 years!